Red Flags

An Illustrated Guide to People We Should've Questioned Sooner

Red Flags

A red flag is an early warning sign: a small signal that something is off before the damage becomes clear. It may be a phrase, a gesture, a tone, a pattern. On its own it seems minor. When it happens repeatedly, it's telling.

The book looks at these patterns on two levels: people and ecosystems. The archetypes that perform them, and the environments that reward and repeat them.

This is a field guide to the warning signs we've learned to ignore. Not just the obvious ones, but the familiar ones: the phrases, gestures, and performances that hint at trouble long before anything breaks. Red flags used to stand out. Now they blend in, masquerading as confidence, urgency, positivity, "strong leadership", or common sense.

They manifest throughout politics, media, and culture, they appear in wellness settings and in work environments. Rather than chase villains, this book maps behaviours: the signals that quietly reshape reality while looking perfectly normal.

Something has shifted. Language drifted away from reality. Certainty travels faster than care. Confidence is rewarded, doubt penalised. Social media didn't invent this, but it accelerated it.

Platforms reward speed over accuracy, repetition over reflection, confidence over competence. Context collapses. Reaction beats consideration. Opinions harden into identities. Algorithms amplify, organise, and scale the pattern.

Facts turn into vibes. Explanations into accusations. Correction into censorship. By the time nuance arrives, the narrative has already settled.

Symbols stop being neutral and become signals: hats, hashtags, fonts, poses, tones. Once you start seeing red flags, you can't unsee them. They're everywhere, wrapped in confidence, urgency, or outrage, fed by systems that reward certainty, conflict, and volume over care or doubt.

I've spent twenty years looking at people through different lensens and in different settings: in meetings and boardrooms, on stages and screens. Patterns reveal themselves. The red flags aren't just out there. They are in us, and even in me.

This book isn't an accusation. It's a mirror.

People

Ecosystems

"Once yo
seeing r
you can't
them."

u start
d flags,
unsee

Pe

ple

The Branding Messiah

The type for whom branding is all about belief rather than strategy. Who relies on slogans, references iconic brands as authority, and frames launches as moments of personal or organisational redemption. Who replaces analysis with aesthetics, interprets failure as insufficient belief, and elevates presentation over substance. And who promotes collaboration rhetorically while consolidating authorship and credit in practice.

What They Say

"What's the one word we want people to feel?"

"It's clean, but it's not elevated."

"We don't sell products, we sell emotions."

"I like it... but I don't love it."

What To Do

Ask where the insight comes from. Moodboards are not sources.

Don't mistake charisma for clarity.

Protect the process. Vision without validation is just a vibe.

Captain Power-Thru

He treats resistance as weakness and exhaustion as a virtue. Every problem is met with more pressure, longer hours, and louder resolve. Reflection becomes delay, limits become excuses. He ignores warnings and people, reframes burnout as commitment, and sees collapse as acceptable fallout. Planning feels soft, rest suspect, and stopping equals failure.

What They Say

"Sleep is for later."

"We can rest after the deadline."

"Let's push a bit harder."

"This isn't the moment to be slowing down."

What To Do

Slow the language down before you slow down the work.

Translate momentum words into measurable actions.

Watch how they react when clarity replaces speed.

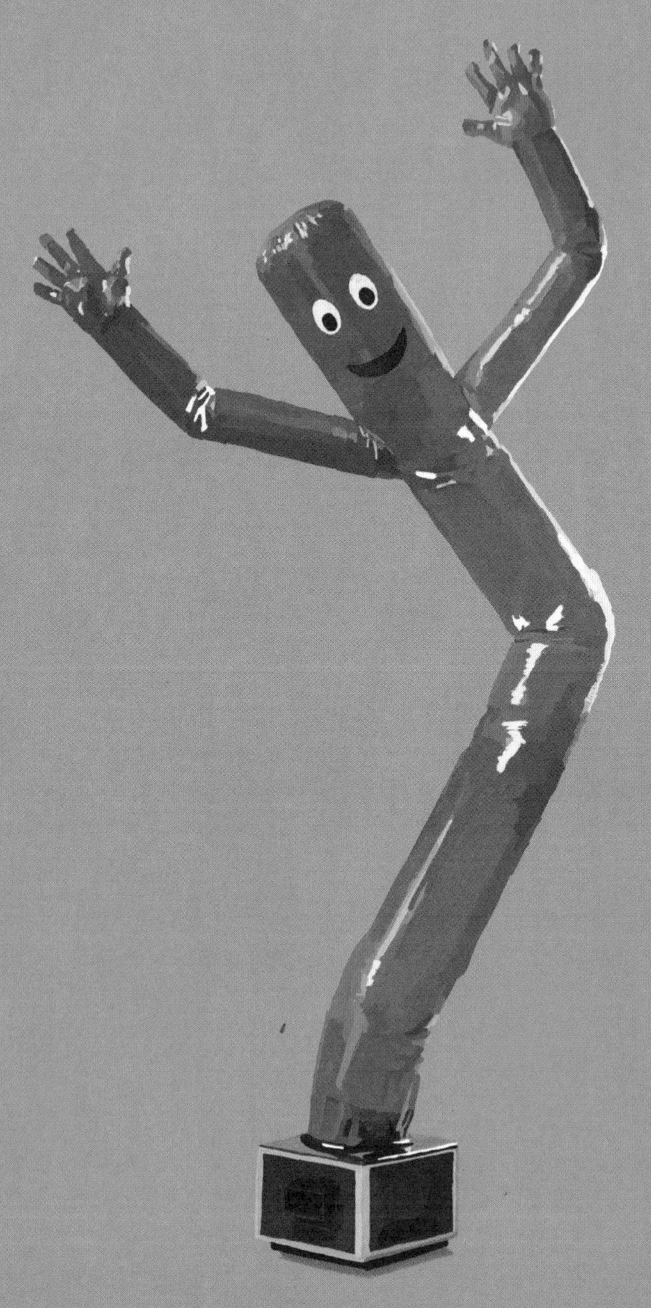

Chief Air Officer

They arrive loud and late, framed as an intervention. Buzzwords lead, with context trailing in their wake. They claim impact without understanding the work, then leave before outcomes appear. All pressure, no reflection. They believe speed is thinking, force is leadership, and breakage is proof of progress — the familiar "move fast and break things" motto.

What They Say

"I've got this."

"Let's take this to the next level."

"I'll unblock things."

"We need better alignment."

What To Do

Don't respond. Attention is the product.

Mute, don't quote. Silence kills reach.

Wait for outcomes. Reality makes the rebuttal.

Follow the "boring" experts instead.

The Scope Creep

Work inflates but it always goes unsaid. Nothing is added openly. It seeps in through comments, side notes, and "quick thoughts" until the project drifts, timelines vanish, and it's still framed as "almost done". Extras rarely arrive as decisions. They appear as small, reasonable additions that quietly change the scope.

What They Say

"Can we just add one more thing?"

"This was kind of implied, right?"

"It's a small tweak."

"We're so close."

What To Do

Pause work when additions appear.

Treat every "small extra" as a decision point.

Close phases before opening new ones.

Let silence do the enforcing.

The Purity Tester

A self-appointed moral inspector who treats ambiguity as guilt and discomfort as proof. They apply shifting standards after the fact, test intentions instead of outcomes, and frame uncertainty as failure. What starts as care ends as control, with nothing safe to say and no room to move.

What They Say

"That's problematic."

"I'm uncomfortable with this."

"This demands caution."

"I expected better from you."

What To Do

Ask about concrete harm, not vibes.

Separate intent from impact, then deal with both.

Refuse retroactive standards. Do not apologise for ambiguity.

Exit conversations once substance runs out.

The Feedback Deflector

They seem open but nothing actually gets through. Feedback is invited, then softened, redirected, or quietly erased, until nothing survives contact. Critique becomes misunderstanding, explanations make way for listening, praise is amplified, and friction filtered out.

What They Say

"I hear you, but..."

"That's interesting, let's park this for now."

"We'll take that onboard."

"It's not a no, it's just not the right time."

What To Do

Ask what will change as a result.

Turn feedback into a written decision.

Set a clear follow-up date or drop it.

Don't be afraid of calling it out when feedback is being deferred.

The Seagull Manager

He shows up loud and uninvited, skips the process, ignores the context, and starts rearranging things he doesn't understand. He adds no value, creating maximum disruption and reframing the resulting chaos as leadership. And then he leaves before anyone can ask questions, convinced that he "guided the team" simply by passing through.

What They Say

"I want to jump in real quick."

"Why wasn't this flagged sooner?"

"Have we looked at the bigger picture?"

"This shouldn't take long."

What To Do

Do not react emotionally to fly-by criticism.

Protect the team from sudden changes in direction.

Push for trade-offs: time, scope, or quality.

Maintain momentum and shield work from interruptions.

The Paper Tiger

He speaks in absolutes, dressing up dominance as discipline and volume as authority. When complexity, doubt, or vulnerability enter the room, he reframes them as weakness and exits with a slogan. He explains emotion through biology or hierarchy, needs an enemy to stay coherent, and treats empathy as a flaw. Being "misunderstood" isn't a failure to him; it's merely evidence that he's operating on a higher plane.

What They Say

"Most men today are lost."

"I don't do feelings. I do focus."

"Weak times create weak men."

"Discipline beats emotion."

What To Do

Do not debate masculinity. It's a suit, not a theory.

Don't take the bait. They feed on reactions, not on truths.

Ask one calm follow-up question. Let them explain themselves into a corner.

"Weak ti
create w

The Paper Tiger

nes
eak men."

The Ghoster

They avoid decisions by disappearing. Silence is their response, distance their excuse. They are just present enough to keep their options open, only to retreat when a commitment is required. By never closing the loop, they let time do the rejecting and keep their hands clean.

What They Say

"Sorry, just saw this."

"Crazy week."

"Let's catch up soon."

"I'll get back to you."

What To Do

Treat silence as an answer.

Do not chase clarity that was intentionally withheld.

Set one date, then close the loop yourself.

Exit conversations when substance runs out.

The Main Character

They move through life as if it's scripted around them. Every room is a stage, every exchange a subplot, every inconvenience a plot twist. Attention isn't sought, it's assumed. Others exist as supporting characters, with conversations that are recentred, shared moments turned into personal lore, and anything that doesn't fit the narrative quietly edited out.

What They Say

"Funny you should mention that, because I..."

"This reminds me of something that happened to me."

"Honestly, my situation is different."

"You wouldn't believe what happened next."

What To Do

Interrupt the narrative, request specifics.

Redirect the focus unapologetically.

Leave early when everything becomes a monologue.

The Energy Vampire

They don't bring drama, they bring gravity. The room doesn't erupt, it slowly dims, and nothing is urgent enough to act on yet always intense enough to demand attention. They occupy emotional space without resolution, turn small issues into ongoing sagas, reject solutions, and keep conversations circling around the same low point.

What They Say

"I don't know why this always happens to me."

"I'm just exhausted."

"It's a lot right now."

"I don't want advice, I just need to vent."

What To Do

Offer solutions once. Stop repeating them.

Do not reward stagnation with attention.

Protect your energy without explaining it.

Leave before the room goes quiet.

The Drama King

We've all heard of the Drama Queen. Meet the Drama King. They mistake alarm for insight and intensity for importance. Everything is urgent. Everything is under threat. Everything is happening right now. If everything is always a crisis, nothing ever actually gets solved.

What They Say

"This is an existential moment in timc."

"People don't understand how serious this is."

"You're missing what's really happening."

What To Do

Name the boundary without shaming.

Redirect the conversation calmly.

Don't let their outrage become your problem.

The Love Bomber

They mistake immediacy for intimacy, oversharing too quickly and turning disclosure into a shortcut to closeness. Personal history arrives unpaced or without consent, framed as honesty. Trauma comes before trust, boundaries are skipped, and cues that say "not here, not now" are ignored in the rush to feel close faster.

What They Say

"I've never felt this before."

"You're different from everyone else."

"I just know things."

"We're the same."

What To Do

Slow the pace deliberately.

Match actions, not declarations.

Watch what happens when you say no.

Stick to your own rhythm.

The Enlightened Centrist

They stay above the mess, proudly unbothered. Every stance is met with a sigh, every conviction with a raised eyebrow, and the refusal to choose is framed as wisdom. By equating all sides, they avoid responsibility, confuse detachment with depth, and ensure nothing actually moves forward.

What They Say

“The truth is probably somewhere in the middle.”

“I can see both sides.”

“People get so emotional about this.”

“It’s more complicated than that.”

What To Do

Ask what they actually stand for.

Refuse false equivalences.

Define when neutrality benefits the status quo.

The Lurker

Always present, never visible. They absorb everything, contribute nothing, and only emerge when it's safe. Silence isn't neutrality, it's a strategy. They look on instead of joining, hoard context without intent, and stay offstage to avoid commitment. Opinions arrive late and fully formed. Accountability never does.

What They Say

"I was about to say the same thing."

"I didn't feel the need to comment."

"I know how this usually ends."

"I've got screenshots."

What To Do

Refuse retroactive alignment. Agreement after consensus is not contribution.

Limit information hoarding. Context without intent becomes leverage.

Keep decisions moving. Momentum exposes the lurkers.

The Conspiritualist

They don't state facts, they generate atmosphere. Truth arrives in fragments and urgency, while paranoia is reframed as awareness. By the time evidence is requested, the fear already feels justified. They ask leading questions, dismiss explanations as naïve, and treat coincidences as proof. Systems give way to villains, and intensity replaces certainty.

What They Say

"You don't think that was random, do you?"

"This goes deeper than you realise."

"Once you see it, you can't unsee it."

"I'm not crazy, I'm early."

What To Do

Separate emotion from evidence. Intensity is not proof.

Don't "connect the dots" for them. Make them do the work and know when to disengage.

Some conversations run on suspicion, not resolution.

The Beige Mom

Everything is calm, curated, and levelled. Choice is framed as chaos, neutrality as virtue, and softness becomes control in a muted palette. Visual harmony replaces lived experience, unpredictability is managed away, and motherhood styled as a lifestyle brand rather than a reality.

What They Say

"We're keeping things neutral."

"It's just more calming this way."

"Bright colours overstimulate them."

"It's about intention."

What To Do

Introduce friction gently. Colour, noise, and mess are not failures.

Ask what's actually needed, not what photographs well.

Don't argue aesthetics. Talk outcomes: play, autonomy, resilience.

Let unpredictability exist without fixing it.

YouTube

The Armchair Expert

A full-time commentator fuelled by livestream stamina and lukewarm takes. He reacts to everything, builds nothing, and treats commentary as an accomplishment. Life advice is dispensed from a swivel chair, politics reduced to culture-war noise, and everything inconvenient is dismissed as "woke". Observation makes way for participation, outrage becomes content, and solutions remain safely theoretical.

What They Say

"I've seen this a thousand times."

"This is why everything kinda sucks now."

"Let's be honest for a second."

"It's actually insane to me."

What To Do

Ask what they've actually built, tried, or risked.

Refuse swivel-chair authority. Commentary is not experience.

Don't accept "objective" claims without evidence. Ask for specifics once.

The Rage Baiter

They don't argue to persuade; they provoke to activate. Outrage is the product, attention the currency, and if you're angry they've already won. Positions are framed in extremes and shift just enough to keep the conflict alive. Backlash is treated as validation, not feedback, because resolution would end the performance.

What They Say

"Seethe."

"Cope."

"Stay pressed."

"Cry harder."

What To Do

Avoid emotional reactions. That's the goal.

Don't quote-tweet the circus.

It's very likely a bot, burner or troll farm, engaged to keep the outrage going.

Starve it of attention. "Cope" dies without an audience.

"Cry hard

The Rage Baiter

er."

The Undecided Voter

They say they're "still deciding" but actually, they weren't paying attention. They hide in a self-made bubble, missing context, nuance, and the plot. When reality catches up, they're shocked that decisions still have consequences. They call disengagement neutrality, skim fragments without context, and act surprised when outcomes feel sudden. They weren't sudden. The signals were just ignored.

What They Say

"I don't really follow politics."

"Both sides have a point."

"It all feels very confusing."

"I didn't think it would matter."

What To Do

Don't over-explain. They weren't listening then, and they won't start now.

Ask what they've actually engaged with.

Stop negotiating with neutrality. When consequences arrive, don't rescue them from surprise.

The Podcast Bro

They don't argue, they nod. Opinions loop until repetition feels like truth. Everyone agrees just enough, every story fits the vibe, and disagreement is kept outside the room. It's a closed circuit of familiar voices, where the same takes are recycled and comfort is mistaken for insight.

What They Say

"That's wild."

"It makes you think."

"There's something to that."

"I don't know, man."

What To Do

Notice the loop. Repetition isn't consensus.

Check who's in the room. A lineup of the usual fringe thinkers is the warning sign.

Track selective outrage. If power gets endless nuance and critics reap instant fury, that's the tell.

"I don't
man. T
wild."

The Podcast Bro

know,
at's

betterhelp

The Tik Tok Therapist

They dispense life advice like discount coupons. Strangers are diagnosed at pace, with confidence outrunning competence. Therapy jargon replaces training, complexity flattens into affirmations, disagreement becomes “unhealed”, and certainty is sold in place of caution.

What They Say

“This is your trauma talking.”

“If this triggered you, there’s work to do there.”

“You’re allowed to feel this way.”

“That’s a nervous system response.”

What To Do

Ask what training backs the advice.

Refuse diagnoses that are delivered as content.

Call it out when language replaces listening.

Step back when care turns into performance.

The Shit Poster

They treat everything as a joke and their timeline as a stage. Nothing is taken seriously, every moment is undercut with a meme or a cheap jab. Anything goes in their jokey culture. Racism, sexism and cruelty all slip in under the guise of irony. If you object, you're the problem. Accountability dies laughing.

What They Say

"Wow, people really can't take a joke anymore."

"I'm obviously being ironic."

"Touch grass."

"I guess free speech is dead."

What To Do

Do not argue about tone.

Ignore the meme, address the claim.

Ask what the joke is. Repeat it back, just louder and dumber.

The Micro Manager

They don't let go. Delegation turns into hovering, trust becomes surveillance. Nothing is ever finished, only temporarily out of reach. Approved work is quietly rewritten, trivial details are overmanaged, and constant involvement is mistaken for value. Control is presented as care, interference as leadership, and the steady presence slowly drains everything of momentum.

What They Say

"Just a quick tweak."

"I'll do it myself, it's faster than explaining it."

"Can you walk me through this again?"

"Let's align on this."

What To Do

Put decisions in writing so changes are visible.

Don't over-explain. Brevity limits interference.

Redirect control requests back to outcomes.

If hovering persists, call it out calmly and reset the boundaries.

The AI-stocrat

A self-crowned noble of the algorithmic age, floating on a cloud of confidence and buzzwords. He speaks fluent hype, treats ethics like optional pop-ups, and sells the aura of AI long before anything actually works. Scale replaces substance, speculation is framed as destiny, and consequences are dismissed with a word salad straight out of a billionaire's playbook.

What They Say

"We're still early."

"The tech will sort itself out."

"Ethics shouldn't slow innovation."

"You'll understand once it scales."

What To Do

Separate hype from reality. Ask what's automated and what is still human labour.

Where did the data come from? If they can't answer, you're the dataset.

Look at who's been replaced and who's protected. The imbalance is intentional.

The Horoscope Hoarder

A cosmic get-out-of-jail-free card disguised as insight. Bad moods, missed deadlines, sudden rudeness? It's never behaviour, it's the stars. Everything becomes planetary interference, safely postponed until the universe "realigns". They talk about cycles and energies, not choices. Responsibility is outsourced to the cosmos, coincidence becomes fate, and consequences are treated like passing weather.

What They Say

"Mercury is in retrograde."

"That's such a Scorpio move."

"The universe is testing me."

"I'm just in a bad cycle right now."

What To Do

Ask which choice they made, not which stars aligned.

Define the behaviour, not the sign.

Refuse cosmic explanations for concrete outcomes.

Bring it back to the now, not to fate.

The Hashtag Activist

Believes posting is participation. Shows up where the algorithm is loudest, armed with a pre-made Instagram slide and a borrowed slogan. They don't organise, they never stay, and they always avoid the boring work. Instead, they document concerns, and then move on. They speak in absolutes and share before reading, mistaking visibility for impact. Commitment lasts one news cycle. When the hashtag fades, so do they.

What They Say

"I'm using my platform."

"Link in bio."

"Amplify this."

"If you're not posting, you're complicit."

What To Do

Don't confuse posting with participation. Look for the people doing the organising offline.

Measure commitment beyond the feed.

Support the groups already doing the work. Join structures that exist instead of chasing the latest hashtag.

"If you're posting, complic

The Hashtag Activist

not
you're
t,"
."

The Life Auditor

Moves through life like a freelance accountant for other people's choices. Keeps mental spreadsheets nobody asked for, tracking tone, timing, and mistakes. Frames this as care, but it's really all about control. Past decisions resurface like unpaid invoices with judgement packaged as concern, correction as help. Forgiveness is rare, forgetting non-existent, and growth is treated as a compliance issue.

What They Say

"I just like clarity."

"Patterns don't lie."

"Let's be honest with ourselves."

"I'm holding space for accountability."

What To Do

Don't justify or over-explain. Because that just adds entries to the ledger.

Keep responses short, focused, and factual. Refuse to engage in retroactive debates about past decisions.

If you find yourself in audit territory, call it out for what it is and close the books.

The Apologist

Never addresses the issue. Always throws you a detour. What about this, what about them? Deflection replaces response. While this may sound nuanced, it causes delays. By the time everything is acknowledged, nothing has been resolved.

What They Say

"This is fine."

"I did not see this coming at all."

"We should be careful about laying blame."

"Never thought I'd be here."

What To Do

Reject moral fog. Accountability isn't an accusation.

Ask who benefits from the delay.

Demand a decision, not reflection.

"Per m
last e

The CC Sniper

y
mail."

The CC Sniper

Turns a private issue into a public situation to gain leverage. Recipients are added not to solve the problem, but to shift power, protect the sender, or apply pressure without open confrontation. The message is always polite. What could be resolved becomes a performance, and by the time everyone has been looped in, the outcome is already set.

What They Say

"Just looping a few people in."

"Per my last e-mail."

"Keeping everyone aligned."

"I thought it was good for leadership to see this."

What To Do

Deflate the audience: ask who actually needs to be involved and why in your reply.

Pull it back to direct contact: suggest taking it offline or resolving the matter 1-to-1.

Close the loop: propose a clear decision or a next step to end the thread.

The Rug Puller

At first, everything looks solid. Clear plans, confident timelines, lots of talk about the long term. Trust comes early, almost naturally. Then people commit and that's when the ground gives way. What follows is never called an exit. It's a pivot. A refocus. A reset. Responsibility slips into process language, consequences become "unfortunate but unavoidable".

What They Say

"This wasn't the original vision I had."

"We need to stay flexible."

"Let's zoom out for a second."

"This is a strategic pivot."

What To Do

Make sure scope, roles, and exits are defined before you invest work and energy that's hard to get back.

Identify the shift early. The longer a "pivot" is not called out, the harder it is to hold anyone accountable.

Keep your options open until trust is earned.

The Labelist

Reduces people to a single label and treats it as the whole story. Context is cut away, complexity discarded. Once you realise it, you're sorted. They speak in categories, not conversations. Individuals become symbols, disagreement becomes betrayal, and nuance is framed as weakness.

What They Say

"That's just who they are."

"You people always do this."

"It's a pattern."

"Typical."

What To Do

Point out the evidence that doesn't fit their category.

Enquire which behaviour, not which group.

Reintroduce any context that they cut away.

Ask what would make them change their mind. Often the answer is nothing.

"You pe
always

The Labelist

ople
do this."

The Truth Muddler

Truth Muddlers don't confront reality. They light fire to create smoke. A small truth. A scary anecdote. A "people are saying". Soon the air is thick with half-facts and suspicion. You can't see what's real, but you know that something feels wrong. They don't need a clean lie. Just enough emotional smoke to hide the facts.

What They Say

"I'm just asking questions."

"People are saying..."

"It's not that simple."

"I'm not saying it's true, but..."

What To Do

Separate fact from feeling. "What part of this is verified, and what part is speculation?"

Ask for sources, not vibes. "Who specifically reported that?"

Name the tactic. "This feels like a lot of suspicion without solid proof."

RAW

The Anti-Vax Cult Leader

They speak the language of protection while sowing doubt, wrapping suspicion in concern and calling it courage. Science is framed as conspiracy, evidence as corruption, and fear sold as independence. Their trick isn't to deny facts outright. Instead, they poison trust so thoroughly that nothing can be proven anymore.

What They Say

"What are they hiding?"

"Do your own research."

"They don't want you to know this."

"Follow the money."

What To Do

Ask for sources that can be independently verified. Vibes aren't scientific proof.

Separate scepticism from cynicism. One questions claims, the other rejects trust entirely.

Refuse endless doubt loops. "Nothing can be proven" is not an argument.

The Threads Televangelist

Delivers absolute truth in vertical reels. Old-school evangelism for a new audience. Certainty is high, context optional, with doctrine moving at algorithm speed. Sacred texts deliver authority, the feed supplies reach. Beliefs are used to lock in gender roles, justify hierarchy, and prescribe how society should function.

What They Say

"Career culture stole motherhood from women."

"Feminism broke the natural balance."

"Roles don't mean inequality."

"Submission isn't weakness. It's wisdom."

What To Do

Separate personal conviction from social control.

Call it out when biology is used as destiny.

Refuse nostalgia-as-proof arguments.

Eco-
syst

ems

Shrinkflation

Shrinkflation is when the price stays the same but the product quietly shrinks. People, effort, time, care, and attention are slowly reduced without this ever being discussed. You still get something, just not what you used to, while expectations of you stay the same. No major conflict, just a gradual shift disguised as being busy or “growth”.

What You'll Hear

“A streamlined product experience.”

“Better for you.”

“Portion-conscious.”

“We listened to our customers.”

What To Do

Treat less for the same price as a new deal. Renegotiate, scale back, or walk. Don’t absorb the loss yourself.

Check what actually changed. Compare the present to the past. What’s slower, thinner, missing, or pushed onto you?

Planned Obsolescence

Designed to fail politely. Looks solid, feels premium, works perfectly, until suddenly it doesn't. Batteries are sealed, parts glued, and updates conveniently incompatible. It's not bad engineering, it's just very good business. Longevity is treated as a bug, replacement as the real feature.

What You'll Hear

"Designed as an integrated system."

"Accessories sold separately."

"Not compatible with newer updates."

"This model is no longer supported."

What To Do

Buy second-hand on purpose.

Choose repairability, not prestige.

Check lifespan before specs.

Avoid sealed ecosystems unless you accept the upgrade cycle.

The Nostalgia K-Hole

Circulates between past classics and present culture. The moment someone's taste was formed is treated as culture's peak. TV used to be better, comedy smarter. Music used to mean something. Seinfeld is held up as proof, not evidence, and anything made after that is dismissed as noise, woke, or inferior by default. The past isn't remembered, it's weaponised.

What You'll Hear

"Why are people so sensitive nowadays?"

"Back then, jokes were savage."

"It wasn't about politics, it was just funny."

"The golden age is over."

What To Do

Point out the survivorship bias. We remember the classics. We tend to forget the oceans of garbage.

Refuse the culture war bait. "Woke" is doing a lot of work for people who stopped paying attention.

Remember: culture didn't decline. It's just curiosity that did.

"Why ar
so sensi
nowada

The Nostalgia K-Hole

people
ive
s?"

Sanewashing

The art of making unhinged ideas sound reasonable, honed on the opinion pages of billionaire-owned media organisations. Calm repetition, a professional tone, and selective framing turn extreme positions into "serious" viewpoints. Context fades, consequences soften, and the focus shifts from the idea itself to the supposed overreaction to it.

What You'll Hear

"The president has floated an unconventional proposal."

"What critics get wrong about..."

"The case for an unpopular opinion."

"Challenging the mainstream narrative."

What To Do

"Floats unconventional proposal" usually means "said something authoritarian out loud".

Separate tone from substance. Calm delivery doesn't make an anti-democratic idea safer.

Say it plainly: this isn't debate, it's normalisation through neutrality.

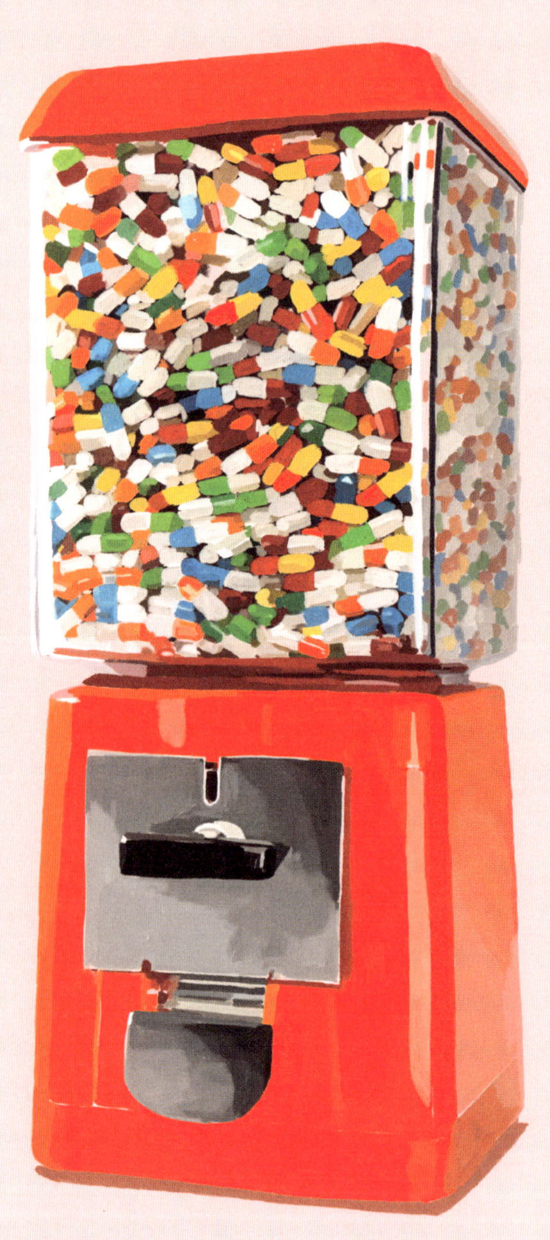

The Wellness Industrial Complex

No checks, no accountability. A parallel health system built on vibes, distrust, and subscriptions. It sells itself as natural and empowering while copying the same extractive logic. Supplements replace evidence, influencers are the new doctors. Health becomes a moral project. Science is optional, regulation is oppression, and the result is an endless slew of powders, pills, and perpetual self-optimization.

What You'll Hear

"Men today have half the testosterone their grandfathers had."

"Modern life is killing your T."

"Plastics. Soy. Screens. Stress."

"This is male optimisation."

What To Do

Separate evidence from marketing. "Clinically proven" isn't a result, it's framing.

Use doctors as translators, not priests. Ask for options, hard numbers, and alternatives.

Avoid absolutism. "No alternative" usually means "no profitable one".

Performative Nationalism

Patriotism stripped of responsibility and repackaged as performance. Flags replace policy, slogans trump civic duty. Love of country becomes loud, selective, and conditional. Critique is framed as betrayal, while the care for institutions, people, or the future quietly fades away. It's nationalism without sacrifice, identity without accountability. A costume that is worn when it fits, discarded when it asks for anything in return.

What You'll Hear

"I guess I'm just proud of where I'm from."

"Stand for the flag."

"Respect the anthem."

"I voted for this."

What To Do

Ask what's being protected, not what's being displayed. Flags are cheap. Policy isn't.

Separate loyalty from silence. Care includes critique.

Blindness isn't devotion.

Follow actions, not aesthetics. Performance ends where responsibility begins.

"I vo
fort

Performative Nationalism

ted
is."

The Grievance Grift

Grievance isn't a reaction anymore. It's a strategy. Hurt becomes branding. Anger becomes community. Every criticism proves persecution. Every setback confirms the script. Solutions would end the story, which is why none are pursued. Outrage creates attention. Attention turns into money. Identity becomes a product, and belonging is sold back to the loyal believers. It's about ensuring it stays broken enough for profit.

What You'll Hear

"They're coming after you, I'm just in the way."`

"This is a witch hunt."

"The system is rigged."

"Nobody's ever been treated worse than this."

What To Do

Protect your own limits. Helping doesn't mean absorbing endless rage.

Offer a way out, not ultimatums. People change their minds when they see alternatives, not when they're cornered.

Discuss what the message does to people's lives.

Clicktatorship

Power sits with platform companies that write the rules, enforce them unilaterally, and change them without notice. Visibility is granted or revoked by ranking systems, moderation policies, and monetisation thresholds that are law, court, and punishment rolled into one. There is no transparency, no due process, no appeal that matters.

What You'll Hear

"We don't take editorial positions."

"This violates our community guidelines."

"We're constantly improving safety."

What To Do

Design for exit. Never build your voice, income, or reach on a single platform. Redundancy is resistance.

Log off on purpose. Attention is the resource.

Stop feeding metrics. No likes, no shares, no hate-clicks. Silence starves systems.

Cultural Colonialism

A system that extracts stories, symbols, and struggle from cultures it claims to support. Tradition becomes aesthetic and resistance becomes branding. Lived experience is curated and displayed at a safe distance. It performs solidarity in soft tones, while real power continues to be gatekept by the usual suspects.

What You'll Hear

"We are giving them a platform."

"This work amplifies marginalised voices."

"Inspired by lived experience."

"We want to start a conversation."

What To Do

Ask who decides, who benefits, and who risks. If those aren't the same people, something's off.

Access is not control. Being included isn't the same as deciding.

If power, money, and decisions remain in the same hands, nothing has changed.

Cry-Bullying

A space where moral language is used to attack and victimhood is used to dodge consequences. Righteous causes serve as cover for personal cruelty. But the minute they feel pushed back, the aggressors reframe themselves as the ones being harmed. Seen across the political spectrum, albeit with different slogans. One side speaks the language of justice and protection, the other the language of freedom and tradition. The script? Always the same.

What You'll Hear

"You attacking me just proves my point."

"Wow, I guess standing up for people makes me a target."

"This is political persecution."

"I'm being silenced by the woke mob."

What To Do

Separate the cause from the conduct. A good slogan does not excuse bad behaviour.

Always refuse the victim flip. Feeling criticised is not the same as being harmed.

Keep standards consistent. Your "side" does not get a moral discount.

PRIME

The Grift-to-Glory Cycle

A playbook perfected by influencer-era figures who turn attention into legitimacy. Controversy is not a mistake, it's the entry point. Shock creates reach. Reach generates money. Money is reframed as success, which is then presented as proof that the criticism never mattered.

What You'll Hear

"This is bigger than me now."

"The numbers don't lie."

"This is just the beginning."

"It's about fuelling the next generation."

What To Do

Ask yourself what you're getting used to. Is it real skill and effort, or just bigger stunts and louder behaviour pitched as success?

Check yourself. Do you feel clearer and more focused, or just wired as you chase the next hit?

Fauxtism

An increasingly common online pattern, where complex neurological traits are flattened into shareable identities. Clinical language is used loosely without context, transforming self-diagnosis into content and neurodiversity into simplified labels. Nuance disappears: spectra give way to labels, traits to diagnoses, and lived reality becomes relatability. This isn't about denying experience. It's about platforms rewarding certainty and labels over care, accuracy, and professional judgment.

What You'll Hear

"Everyone's on the spectrum."

"Diagnosis is a privilege."

"It's not a disorder, it's an identity."

"If it resonates, it's real."

What To Do

Encourage guidance, not certainty. Professional help isn't oppression, it's context.

Keep the focus on those who need support most. Visibility shouldn't dilute care.

Distinguish exploration from conclusion. Learning about traits isn't the same as settling on a diagnosis.

"Every
on the
spectr

Fauxtism

one's

m."

The Familiarity Machine

When repeated exposure morphs into the feeling of knowing someone. Faces, voices, routines, and confessions are so common on our screens that recognition breeds a relationship. Parasocial behaviour is what makes this work. We form one-sided emotional bonds with people who don't know we exist, projecting closeness where there is only visibility. The creator performs presence. The viewer supplies intimacy.

What You'll Hear

"I feel like I really know them."

"They're just so genuine."

"I've followed them for years."

"They would never do that."

What To Do

Remind yourself: visibility is not the same as a relationship.

Notice when you're filling in blanks with assumptions.

Separate performance from personal connection.

Ask what you really know beyond what's shown.

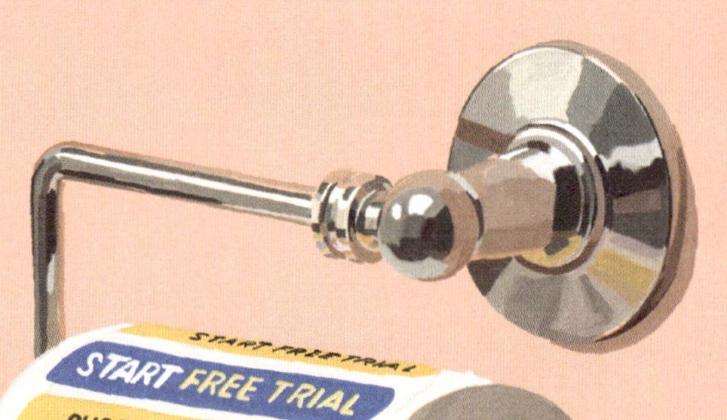
START FREE TRIAL
START FREE TRIAL
SUBSCRIBE MONTHLY
UNLOCK PREMIUM
PAY TO UNLOCK
ACCEPT ALL COOKIES
WATCH AD TO SKIP
UPGRADE TO CONTINUE
CANCEL LATER
REMOVE LIMITS
PRO ONLY
AUTO-RENEW ENABLED
ALLOW TRACKING
SKIP WITH ADS
BOOST ENGAGEMENT
PAY TO UNLOCK
GET PRO BUNDLE
BUY EXTRA SLOT

Enshittification

A term coined by Cory Doctorow. The predictable decay of platforms after they've captured their users. What starts out as useful and generous becomes gradually mired with ads, fees, friction, and dark patterns. Value is extracted and alternatives vanish. The experience worsens by design, not accident. By the time it's unbearable, leaving is the hardest part.

What You'll Hear

"Introducing a new pricing tier."

"Based on your activity."

"This feature is moving to Pro."

"We've updated our terms."

What To Do

Export your data before you need to. Leaving gets harder over time, by design.

Support alternatives while they're still usable. Competition dies quietly.

Pay for tools that respect you. Free usually means future extraction.

The Attention Economy

A system where human focus is the primary commodity. Platforms compete, not to inform or enrich but to capture and hold attention as long as possible, rewarding whatever provokes the strongest reaction. Depth, nuance, and truth lose to speed, outrage, and distraction, because attention, once hooked, can always be sold.

What You'll Hear

"Trending now."

"Don't miss out."

"Based on engagement."

"Hot take."

What To Do

Choose sources, not feeds. Algorithms optimise reaction, not relevance.

Reclaim boredom. Silence is where thinking makes a comeback.

Notice emotional hooks. If it spikes outrage or anxiety instantly, you're the product.

Bothsides Bullshit

A rhetorical strategy that treats unequal ideas as equally valid in the name of "balance". Facts and falsehoods are placed on the same scale, accountability dissolves into debate, and power differences quietly disappear. Behind the veneer of bothsides balance, a clear agenda advances while neutrality is performed.

What You'll Hear

"Both sides have a point."

"The truth is probably somewhere in the middle."

"It's much more complicated than that."

"Everyone's biased."

What To Do

Ask what's being equated. Not all arguments deserve equal weight.

Call out power differences. Neutral language often erases responsibility.

Interrupt the false symmetry. Ask: equal how exactly? Evidence, harm, power, and intent are not interchangeable.

Bettingfication

A system where risk is gamified and everything becomes a wager. Sports, finance, politics, even personal choices are framed as odds, streaks, and wins, training people to think in terms of bets rather than consequences. When life is treated like a sportsbook, losing no longer feels exceptional and responsibility becomes optional.

What You'll Hear

"All in."

"High risk, high reward."

"What are the odds?"

"It's basically a lock."

What To Do

Track losses, not wins. Systems sell streaks and forget damage.

Refuse gamified language. Not everything is a play, a bet, or a score.

Reassert responsibility. Risk taken casually is usually risk outsourced.

Quality
Learing Center
1-800-FRAUD

The Slopaganda

It's not about being right, it's about being everywhere. Push content fast and often, flood the feed before anyone has the time to think. Volume beats clarity. Outrage keeps it going, engagement keeps it profitable. Nuance slows things down, so it gets cut, and accuracy comes second to reach. It doesn't need to make sense. It just needs to stay in front of you.

What You'll Hear

"I broke the algorithm."

"This is blowing up."

"I speak for millions."

"They're trying to suppress this."

What To Do

Deflate metric myths. "I broke the algorithm" is scale cosplay. Reach is not impact.

Track patterns, not claims. One phrase means nothing. Repetition tells you everything.

Withhold amplification. Engagement completes the strategy. Silence interrupts it.

"I bro
algor

The Slopaganda

ke the
thm."

The Race to the Bottom

Standards are deliberately lowered to remain competitive. Quality, ethics, pay, safety, or truth are treated as optional once someone else undercuts first. Every step down is justified as realism, pressure, or survival. No one claims to want it, but everyone participates. The system doesn't collapse in one move, it degrades by imitation. What starts as compromise ends as the new baseline.

What You'll Hear

"This is the market now."

"It's just temporary."

"We'll fix it later."

"At least we're still in the game."

What To Do

Ask what becomes impossible once this is normalised.

Set a floor and treat it as non-negotiable.

Reward those who hold the line, not those who undercut it.

If surviving means lowering your standards, question the system, not yourself.

Aipac

Astroturfing

A manufactured show of public support disguised as grassroots momentum. Organisations, brands, or political actors simulate “ordinary people” to create the illusion of widespread agreement. Hashtags, testimonials, comments, and outrage are carefully seeded, amplified, and coordinated from the top, then presented as spontaneous demand from below.

What You'll Hear

“This isn’t a campaign.”

“No one told us to post this.”

“We all just feel this.”

“It’s organic.”

What To Do

Look for coordination signals. Identical language, timing, hashtags, or talking points are tells.

Check origins, not volume. Ten loud accounts aren’t a movement.

Follow the money and infrastructure.

Security Theatre

A language of control built from symbols rather than outcomes. Visibility replaces effectiveness, and reassurance becomes a proxy for protection. The system appears busy, confident, and intact.

What You'll Hear

"We're taking decisive action."

"This sends a strong signal."

"If you oppose this, you're irresponsible."

"The people demand this."

What To Do

Separate visibility from effectiveness. Uniforms, fences, patrols, announcements are not evidence.

Track cost versus benefit. Security theatre is often expensive reassurance.

Refuse false binaries. Security and rights are not opposites by default.

The Memory Hole

A result of limited attention combined with a constant flow of new information. Headlines make way for newer headlines. Promises, scandals, and policy shifts move down the feed as the next development takes priority. More often than not, they are not revisited. When the pace of information outstrips the time needed to evaluate it, follow-up weakens. Issues that are not actively tracked tend to fade from public focus.

What You'll Hear

“That was a long time ago.”

“We’ve moved on.”

“I don’t recall that.”

“Why bring this up now?”

What To Do

Keep a timeline. Memory beats momentum.

Resurface patterns, not isolated scandals.

Don’t let speed replace accountability.

Debate Battle Royale

It has all the makings of an open dialogue but it's actually competitive theatre. One person in the centre. Multiple challengers rotating around them. Fast exchanges, sharp comebacks, audience tension. In a Debate Battle Royale, survival replaces understanding. Confidence reads as credibility. Whoever "holds their own" appears right, even when nothing has been properly examined. Nuance doesn't lose, it just runs out of time.

What You'll Hear

"Answer the question, yes or no."

"That's not what I asked."

"So you can't defend that?"

"Be honest."

What To Do

Slow down the pace on purpose.

Refuse false yes-or-no traps on complex issues.

Ask for definitions before defending positions.

Separate performance pressure from the actual topic.

The Social Media Mirage

The illusion that what you see online is reality, when it's actually a curated performance shaped by algorithms and selective sharing. Feeds amplify confidence, drama, and certainty while cropping out context, doubt, and nuance. Repetition makes things feel common. Engagement makes them seem important. Visibility is equated with truth. The danger isn't that it's fake. It's that it's convincing enough to distort how we see the world.

What You'll Hear

"We're just living our best life."

"So grateful for this journey."

"Hard work pays off."

"Blessed."

What To Do

Always assume the feed is staged, not representative.

Look for what is never shown: stress, debt, conflict, boredom.

Separate wealth signals from actual stability.

Don't compare your life to a highlight reel.

"Bles

The Social Media Mirage

sed."

Dog-Whistling

Dog-Whistling is communication designed to be heard twice. On the surface it sounds neutral. Beneath it, coded language signals belonging to insiders while denying intent to everyone else. It spreads controversial ideas quietly, safely, and repeatedly.

What You'll Hear

"We have to protect our way of living."

"We can't say that anymore."

"Common sense immigration policy."

"You know what I mean."

What To Do

Replace feeling with criteria. "What are the actual performance metrics?"

Separate security concerns from identity insinuations. Translate euphemisms into plain language.

Don't overreact theatrically. Outrage helps them retreat into innocence. Precision traps them in clarity.

In Loving Memory of
RESPONSIBILITY

Management Consultification

Strategies built on thin air, packaged in expensive slides. Problems are reframed, timelines extended, and risks redistributed. Nothing is owned, everything is “aligned”. The people presenting the plan won’t have to live with it. When it fails, they simply rotate to the next engagement, higher fee, same framework. All that remains are the deck and the consequences.

What You'll Hear

“This requires transformation.”

“Let’s align stakeholders first.”

“We’re defining the roadmap.”

“This is industry best practice.”

What To Do

Ask who owns the outcome when the plan fails.

Demand concrete action with a name and a deadline.

Follow results, not slides. If the framework grows but nothing moves, stop the process.

Sausagefication

When complex reality is processed into simplified, emotionally charged content for easy consumption. A logic shaped by reality TV and infotainment, where drama, personality, and narrative replace depth because they hold attention and generate revenue. Like with a sausage, you can't see what's in it. Nuance and uncertainty are ground down into clean storylines with heroes and villains that are easier to sell than to understand.

What You'll Hear

"Can we make it more dramatic?"

"This needs a villain."

"That won't trend."

"Too slow, too smart."

What To Do

Compare multiple outlets, especially those with different incentives.

Track who gets airtime and who never does.

Watch what disappears after the cycle moves on.

Don't let repetition become a stand-in for truth.

Sportswashing

Power enters sport quietly, through repetition and access. FIFA tournaments turn systemic abuse into celebration. Oligarch club ownership shifts from scandal to strategy to background fact. Sport feels apolitical, so the politics slide through unchecked. Each event lowers resistance, each deal normalises the contradiction. Nothing is ever confronted directly, it's merely absorbed. By the time it's noticed, it's already treated as how the game works.

What You'll Hear

"Sport should unite, not divide."

"This isn't political."

"Let's focus on the game."

"Ownership doesn't affect performance."

What To Do

Follow the money, not the messaging.

Treat ceremonies and prizes as signals, not solutions.

Separate athletes from owners, sponsors, and institutions.

Refuse the "just sport" framing. It's the shield.

Vaporware

A future announced before it exists. The demo standing in for a working product. Promises doing the work of delivery. Vaporware thrives on spectacle. The headset works. The trailer looks stunning. The keynote is flawless. The world inside the headset, however, is mostly empty. The announcement is the achievement.

What You'll Hear

"This is the future."

"We're still early."

"You just don't see the vision yet."

"It's about positioning."

What To Do

Ask who uses it daily, not who invested in it.

Separate demo from delivery.

Follow utility, not valuation.

If it solves a real problem, it won't need a keynote to prove it.

Vice Signalling

The performance of cruelty as identity. Where virtue signalling advertises goodness, vice signalling advertises transgression. It's the public flaunting of harsh, taboo, or dehumanising views to appear tough, authentic, or rebellious to a specific in-group.

What You'll Hear

"If you don't like it, leave the country."

"Libtard."

"Low-IQ take."

"NPC energy."

What To Do

Don't rise to the bait. Say what you need to say, then step away. Don't compete for dominance.

Don't argue with the loudest person in the room. Talk to the people who are quietly watching.

"I'm on
connec
the dot

The Author Without a Clue

y
ting
s"
s.

The Author Without a Clue

The final red flag: me. If someone sounds very sure they've figured things out, take it lightly. Look at patterns long enough and you start believing you stand above them. This book isn't proof of insight, just proof of attention. I noticed things, collected them, and shaped them into language. That doesn't mean I'm right. It only means I spent time looking. If this book resonates with you, good. Use it. Steal from it. If it doesn't, also good. Close it. Walk away.

What You'll Hear

"I'm not saying I'm right, but..."

"I just want people to think critically."

"I'm only connecting the dots."

"This book isn't about me." (It is.)

What To Do

Look for the blind spots they don't name. Real thinkers flag their own limits.

Don't outsource your judgement.

Use the lens, don't live inside it. If it stops being useful, walk away. No ideology deserves a subscription plan.

Sources

BOOKS

The Echo Machine
David Pakman
How right-wing extremism has led to the fall of critical thinking and rise of reactionary politics and what we can do about it to save our democracy.

The Sociopath Next Door
Martha Stout
An astonishing, chilling and appallingly useful guide to recognising conscienceless individuals.

Why Does He Do That
Lundy Bancroft
A guide to understanding abusive men, recognising warning signs, and navigating dangerous relationships.

People of the Lie
M. Scott Peck
Cases where behaviour isn't explained by illness, but by intentional harm.

Power: A Radical View
Steven Lukes
How power operates, including the ways it shapes what people see and accept.

The 48 Laws of Power
Robert Greene
48 recurring patterns of power, drawn from history, philosophy, and real-world examples.

The Status Game
Will Storr
Status, not power or money, drives human behaviour. On human life and how to play it.

The Unaccountability Machine
Dan Davies
Why big systems make terrible decisions, and how the world lost its mind.

Why We're Polarized
Ezra Klein
How identity-driven polarisation reshaped American politics and created feedback loops pushing the system toward crisis.

The Gaslight Effect
Robin Stern
How to spot and survive the hidden manipulation others use to control your life.

Careless People
Sarah Wynn-Williams
An insider's view on Facebook's culture. Power, growth at all costs, and the human consequences behind the platform.

In Sheep's Clothing
George K. Simon
Understanding and dealing with manipulative people.

Work Won't Love You Back
Sarah Jaffe
How devotion to our jobs keeps us exploited, exhausted, and alone.

Profiles in Ignorance
Andy Borowitz
How America's politicians got dumb and dumber.

Bullshit Jobs
David Graeber
The rise of pointless work, and what we can do about it.

Culture Warlords
Talia Lavin
A journey into the dark web of white supremacy.

The Attention Merchants
Tim Wu
The epic scramble to get inside our heads.

The Chaos Machine
Max Fisher
The inside story of how social media rewired our minds and our world.

Empire of AI
Karen Hao
Dreams and nightmares in Sam Altman's OpenAI.

The Age of Surveillance Capitalism
Shoshana Zuboff
How companies like Google and Meta turned human behaviour into data, creating a new form of capitalism.

Technopoly
Neil Postman
A critique of how technology reshapes culture, often in ways we fail to notice or question.

Burn Book
Kara Swisher
A front-row account of tech's rise. Big personalities, bigger egos, and the culture that built the industry.

You Are Not So Smart
David McRaney
An entertaining illumination of the stupid beliefs that make us feel wise.

Enshittification
Cory Doctorow
Why everything suddenly got worse and what to do about it.

The Sirens' Call
Chris Hayes
How attention became the world's most endangered resource.

PODCASTS, YOUTUBE & VISUAL SYSTEMS

American Friction
A UK podcast analysing US politics from an external perspective, focusing on media narratives, political strategy, and contemporary developments.
Hosts: Jacob Jarvis, Chris Jones and Nikki McCann Ramirez.

Pod Save America, Pod Save the World and Offline
Podcasts examining political communication, international affairs, and media narratives, with an emphasis on strategy and messaging.
Hosts: Jon Favreau, Jon Lovett, Tommy Vietor, Dan Pfeiffer and Ben Rhodes.

The Ezra Klein Show
A podcast exploring political and social systems through in-depth interviews and analytical discussion.

On with Kara Swisher
A podcast featuring interviews with leaders in technology, media, and politics, focusing on power and decision-making.

The Rest Is Politics
A podcast analysing political strategy, communication, and institutional dynamics in the UK and internationally.
Hosts: Alastair Campbell and Rory Stewart.

The Bulwark Podcast
A political podcast examining democratic institutions and authoritarian trends from a conservative perspective.
Host: Tim Miller.

The David Pakman Show
A daily political program analysing media narratives, rhetoric, and current events.

Secular Talk
A political commentary show focusing on policy, media critique, and ideological analysis.
Host: Kyle Kulinski.

Hysteria
A podcast discussing politics through the lenses of culture, identity, and gender.
Hosts: Erin Ryan and Alyssa Mastromonaco.

Behind the Bastards
A podcast exploring historical and contemporary figures and the systems they operate within, focusing on power, ideology, and systemic harm.
Host: Robert Evans.

Raging Moderates
A political podcast offering analysis that avoids partisan alignment, focusing on nuance and critical evaluation.
Hosts: Scott Galloway and Jessica Tarlov.

The Majority Report with Sam Seder
A daily political show analysing media narratives, power structures, and ideological framing.

I've Had It
A podcast providing commentary on culture and everyday issues through a direct and conversational format.
Hosts: Jennifer Welch and Angie "Pumps" Sullivan.

Elephant Graveyard
A podcast examining internet culture, digital media, and online behaviour, with a focus on trends and systems.

Hasan Piker
A live-streamed political commentary format analysing current events, media narratives, and online culture in real time.

Better Offline
A podcast critiquing the technology industry, focusing on platform dynamics, venture capital, and digital narratives.
Host: Ed Zitron.

Origin Story
A podcast exploring the historical development of political ideas and concepts, including their contemporary interpretations.
Hosts: Dorian Lynskey and Ian Dunt.

WRITERS & THINKERS

Heather Cox Richardson
An American historian and professor at Boston College specialising in 19th-century American political and economic history, with a focus on democratic institutions and political narratives.

Anne Applebaum
An American journalist and historian known for her work on the history of Communism and the development of civil society in Central and Eastern Europe.

F.D. Signifier
An American YouTube video essayist and cultural critic focusing on Black media, masculinity, and the social dynamics of online culture.

David Frum
A Canadian-American political commentator and former speechwriter for President George W. Bush, currently a senior editor at The Atlantic.

Timothy Snyder
An American historian specialising in the history of Central and Eastern Europe, the Soviet Union, and the Holocaust.

Rebecca Solnit
An American writer and activist whose work addresses politics, culture, and social change.

Anand Giridharadas
An American author, journalist, and political analyst known for his critiques of elite-driven narratives of social change.

Zeynep Tüfekçi
A Turkish-American sociologist whose work focuses on social media, media ethics, and the societal impact of emerging technologies such as artificial intelligence and big data.

Shoshana Zuboff
An American scholar who examines how digital technologies reshape work, power, and capitalism, particularly through data-driven economic models.

Byung-Chul Han
A South Korean-born German philosopher whose work critiques neoliberalism, digital culture, and their effects on society and individual behaviour.

Ta-Nehisi Coates
An American writer and journalist known for his work on race, history, and the social and political experiences of African Americans.

James C. Scott
An anthropologist and political scientist who studied state power, peasant societies, and the subtle ways people resist control.

Jonathan V. Last
A prominent conservative journalist, author, and editor at The Bulwark known for analysing American politics, demographic trends, and pop culture.

Bill Kristol
An American political analyst focusing on conservative politics.

Jamelle Bouie
An American journalist and columnist analysing US politics, institutions, and historical power structures.

Rutger Bregman
A Dutch historian and writer exploring economic systems, inequality, and alternative social models.

Keeanga-Yamahtta Taylor
An American academic examining housing, structural inequality, and social movements.

For an up-to-date list and more red flags subscribe to our substack

Thanks

This book exists thanks to the people who kept me grounded while I was staring too long at the mess.

Thank you to my wife, Magali, and my kids, Nolan and Saul, for keeping me real, sharp, and occasionally pulling me back into the actual world.

Thank you to the Luster team for believing in this project and giving it the space it needed to truly find its shape. Special thanks to Dettie, Sandy, Hadewijch and Katya for the constructive feedback, the careful reading, and the rounds of questioning that made this book better.

And finally, to the authors, journalists, podcasters, and independent voices pushing against the slop, the noise, and the algorithmic machines: thank you for doing the work, asking better questions, and proving that clarity still matters.

About the author:
Bart Kiggen is a visual storyteller based in Antwerp. His work sits at the intersection of image, culture, and systems, often examining how aesthetics, language, and power shape what we accept as normal. Red Flags is his latest project, combining illustration and critical observation into a visual field guide for the present moment.

Red Flags

Illustrations, writing and design
Bart Kiggen

Text editing
Sandy Logan
Hadewijch Ceulemans

D/2026/12.005/2
ISBN 9789460583995
NUR 734

info@lusterpublishing.com
lusterpublishing.com
@lusterbooks

Printed in Europe.

Subscribe to our newsletter
for new book alerts and a look
behind the scenes: